embroidery

for little miss crafty

embroidery
for little miss crafty

Projects and Patterns
to Create and Embellish

Helen Dardik

Walter Foster Publishing, Inc.
3 Wrigley, Suite A
Irvine, California 92618
www.walterfoster.com

table of contents

Crafty Cravings

Do you love crafting things? Are you obsessed with personalizing your accessories and surroundings? If the answer to these questions is "yes," you're going to adore this book!

Don't worry if you have never picked up a needle and thread. This is a guide for beginners, and it will ease you into the wonderful world of embroidery. All of the projects in this book are fast, easy, and fun to make. Best of all, embroidery is a way to turn any ordinary old thing into something fabulous and stylish. We're not just talking about kitchen towels and handkerchiefs here. From a cell phone and greeting card to a plain pair of jeans—anything can use a personal touch! Embroidery projects can also make great and unique gifts.

Well, what are you waiting for, Little Miss Crafty? Turn the page and let's get to it!

tools you'll need

Let's just say you are in luck! Embroidery is one of the least expensive hobbies you can take up. You probably already have most of the supplies needed for the projects in this book, and the rest you can easily find in any craft or fabric store without spending tons of money.

needles

You'll need crewel/embroidery needles. These are basic sharp needles, and they should be about the same thickness as your floss. You'll also need regular sewing needles.

floss

For most of the projects in this book, you'll need regular floss (DMC® is recommended). It has six strands and comes in quite a variety of colors. You can also use metallic thread, wool yarn, or thin ribbon.

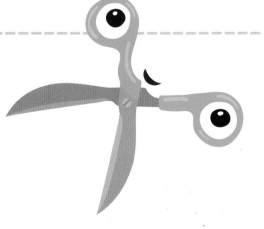

scissors

There is no need for special embroidery scissors. A small pair of sharp scissors will do just fine. You'll become good friends with this trusty little tool.

thread cards

These cardboard cutouts will come in handy when organizing and storing excess thread. You can even make your own cards and decorate them with your unique designs.

fabric

The majority of the projects in this book call for 100% cotton fabric and fun, colored felt. Really, you can embroider on almost any fabric, but keep in mind that thick, sturdy fabric is easiest to work with. I recommend using items you already own that are in desperate need of personality (like plain jeans, felt scarves, iPod cases, etc.).

air-vanishing pen

An air-vanishing or water-soluble pen is helpful if you want to transfer a design using a light table or window.

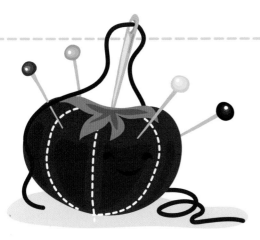

pin cushion

It's a good idea to keep all of your needles and pins in one place where you can easily spot them. A stray pin lying around can make for a very unpleasant and painful surprise!

embroidery hoop

This useful tool will keep your fabric in place as you stitch. You should start with 3" and 5" plastic hoops. Open up the hoop and lay your fabric over the solid inner hoop, making sure your pattern is centered. Next, place the adjustable outer hoop on top, press down, and tighten the screw. Be careful not to tighten too much, or you might permanently stretch the fabric.

templates

Having trouble coming up with embroidery designs? Use the templates at the back of this book! If you need to enlarge a pattern, simply use a photocopier or computer scanner. Once it's the desired size, you can use the techniques on pages 68–69 to transfer it onto your fabric.

extras

You might also need buttons, ribbons, or cardstock. Experiment with different materials to add your unique touch to a project.

choosing colors

There are no strict rules for color selection, but you may try some common combinations inspired by the color wheel. *Complementary colors* (colors directly opposite each other) make great contrasts, and *analogous colors* (colors close to each other) create a harmonious mood.

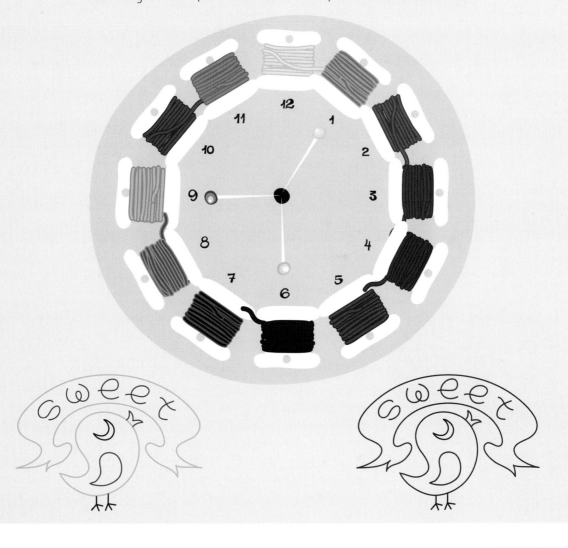

basic stitches

Now that you have all of your tools and materials, it's the perfect time to learn the basic stitches that you'll use to bring your embroidery projects to life. Put a scrap piece of fabric into your embroidery hoop and practice the following stitches. The a, b, and c indicate the order in which the needle goes in and out of the fabric. When you feel confident with these stitches, you can begin the projects!

straight stitch

This stitch is also called the dashed stitch. It's easy peezee!

a. Bring the needle up from the back of the fabric to the front.
b. Then, insert the needle into the fabric approximately ¼" farther and gently pull the thread through. Repeat for the length of your line.

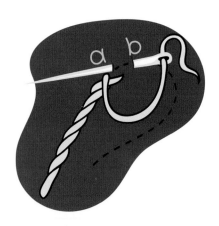

stem stitch

Also known as an outline stitch, the stem stitch is great for curving lines.

a. Work from left to right, making regular small stitches along the line. The thread always emerges on the left side of the previous stitch.
b. The needle comes up between the first two points of the stitch. Make sure that stitches are all evenly spaced as you stitch along your line. The thread loop falls below each of the stitches as you work.

satin stitch

The satin stitch is many straight stitches sewn close together, side-by-side (but not overlapping) to fill out a shape.

a. Bring the needle up at one side of the shape's outline.
b. Insert the needle at the opposite edge of the shape.
Repeat side-by-side stitches until you have a solid shape.

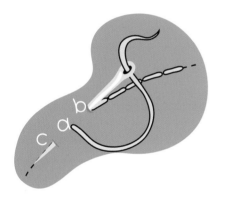

back stitch

This stitch is great for a clean continuous line.

a. Draw the needle up through the fabric and make a short straight stitch backward along your line.
b. With the needle in back of the work, take a long stitch forward to the front of the piece.
c. Backward stitch once again up to the stitch before. Keep stitches equal in length with no gaps left between them.

lazy daisy stitch

The lazy daisy stitch is an easy way to make adorable flowers. It's similar to the chain stitch on page 12.

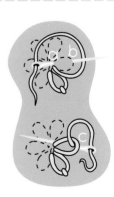

a. Make a small loop of floss and push the needle down through the fabric close to where you started.
b. Bring the needle up just inside the loop.
c. It goes down again just outside the loop, holding it in place.

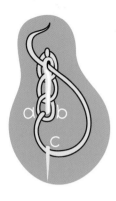

chain stitch

This stitch can be used alone to make pretty chain lines or in rows as a filling.

a. Bring the needle through from the back to the front of the fabric.
b. Through the same hole, insert the needle from the front to the back so the floss is under the needle.
c. To end, anchor the loop with a small lazy daisy stitch.

french knot

These little knots will give your project a fun texture. They are easy to do, and once you master them, you'll be looking for reasons to use them!

a. Pull the floss up through the fabric.
b. Hold the floss down to the fabric with your thumb and encircle the floss around the needle two times.
c. Still holding the floss down, pull up gently and allow a knot to form on top of the fabric.
d. Push the needle down into the fabric close to where the thread first emerged.

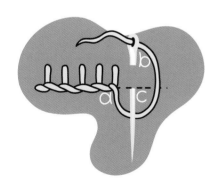

blanket stitch

This stitch is great for creating decorative borders and sewing two sides together.

a. Bring the needle up through the fabric at the lower line.
b. Insert the needle on the upper line with the needle perpendicular to the lower line.
c. Push the needle back through the lower line. With the thread under the needle, pull the thread to form a loop.

✳ To finish, take a small stitch to the back to secure the last loop.

split stitch

You can create so many things with this simple split stitch! It's great for outlining your designs.

a. Make a single straight stitch.
b. Bring the needle up for the next stitch through the center of the previous stitch, "splitting" the first stitch in the middle.

✴ You can stitch two or more lines in this style side-by-side to make extra thick lines or to fill out spaces (instead of using a satin stitch).

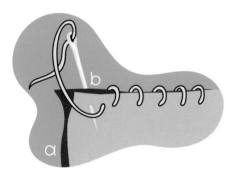

overcast stitch

This easy stitch is used to neatly finish edges and prevent fraying.

a. Secure fabric edges firmly together.
b. Bring the needle from one side to the other over the edge and back underneath.

seed stitch

This stitch is great for shading in outlined areas. It is made out of many short straight stitches going in random directions. You can mark random lines with a fabric pen and then follow them, or you can just dive right in and go stitch crazy.

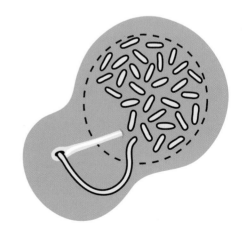

crafty cover

Add a personal touch or special flair to your journal or favorite book with this easy-to-make felt cover. All you need is a journal or book, some felt, and a bit of floss.

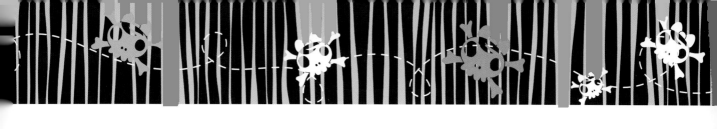

satin stitch

french knot

back stitch

keep Out!

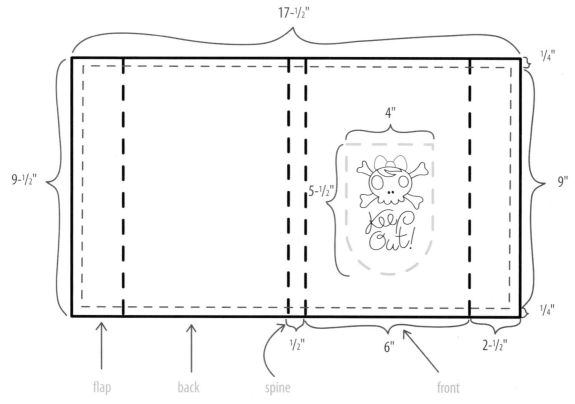

17-1/2"

1/4"

4"

9-1/2"

5-1/2"

9"

keep Out!

1/4"

flap

back

spine

1/2"

6"

front

2-1/2"

Step 1

Measure your journal. For example, if your book is 9" (W) x 6" (L) with a $1/2$" spine, its total measurement would be 9" (W) x 12-$1/2$" (L). Add 5" to the length for the flaps (2-$1/2$" on each side) and $1/2$" all around to give you space for stitching it together (see the diagram on page 17). Cut your red felt accordingly: in this case it's 9-$1/2$" (W) x 17-$1/2$" (L).

Step 2

Unfold the journal and place it in the middle of the felt rectangle. Fold the extra felt on the sides over the journal cover to make the flaps; close the journal. Use pins to hold the flaps in place and gently remove the journal. Use a simple running stitch through the top and bottom of the journal to secure the flaps and to create a decorative border.

Step 3

Now start on the pocket. First, cut out a 4" x 5-1/2" rectangle from white felt and round off the bottom. Next, transfer the pattern on page 71 onto the felt (see pages 68–69 for more on pattern transfers). Embroider the "Keep out!" skull and crossbones design using the back stitch. Use a french knot stitch for the nostrils, and fill out the eye sockets with the satin stitch. Go over the top of the pocket with the overcast stitch.

Step 4

Once you've finished embroidering the pocket, center it on the front of the cover. Use pins to secure the pocket in position. Attach the sides and bottom of the pocket to the journal cover using the running stitch. While you're attaching the pocket, make sure that you keep the flap out of the way with your hand so you don't sew it shut.

You could also:
Add a ribbon bookmark to the back flap.

✳ Or if you'd like to save time, simply skip the pocket and stitch a design directly onto the cover. Make sure you choose a floss color that stands out against the color of the felt cover.

cell cozy

This unique case makes a stylish accessory and protects your cell phone or MP3 player from bumps and scratches.

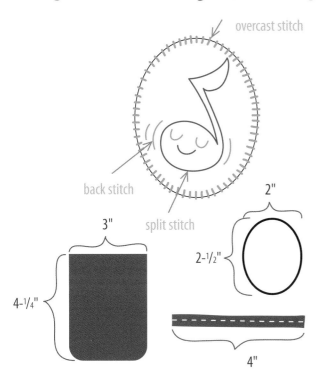

overcast stitch

back stitch

split stitch

3"

4-¼"

2"

2-½"

4"

materials

You'll need:

- ✳ Ruler
- ✳ 2 colors of felt
- ✳ Scissors
- ✳ Needle & pins
- ✳ 3 colors of floss
- ✳ One ½" button
- ✳ Air-vanishing pen
- ✳ 4" ribbon
- ✳ Key ring

Step 1

Measure and cut two rectangles of red felt 4-¼" (W) x 3" (L). Place them on top of each other and round out the bottom corners with scissors.

Step 2

Measure and cut two rectangles of white felt 2-½" (W) x 2" (L). Place them on top of each other and round off all the corners so you have two ovals.

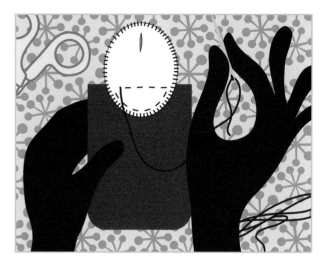

Step 3

Transfer the music note design (page 73) onto one of the white felt ovals and embroider using mostly the split stitch and back stitch for a nice continuous line. Place the finished embroidered white oval on one of the red felt pieces about 1/2" from the bottom, and secure it with pins. Using the overcast stitch, sew the two pieces together. Next, center and attach your button near the top.

Step 4

Take the second oval and run an overcast stitch all around the border. With the air-vanishing pen, draw a 1/2" vertical line in the center, 1/2" from the bottom of the oval, and cut this 1/2" slit for the button hole. Next, center and pin this oval to the unused piece of red felt so it covers 1" of the top. Sew the two pieces together using a simple running stitch.

designs that will also work:

Step 5

Place the decorated pieces of felt back-to-back so that the white felt pieces face out. Secure them with pins, and sew the sides and rounded bottom together using white floss and the blanket stitch.

Step 6

Fold the ribbon in half and attach it to the inner right side of the pocket. Only stitch on one piece of red felt, so the pocket stays open. Slip a key ring onto the ribbon, place your cell phone inside the case, button it up, and you're good to go!

✖ You can simplify this project by embroidering directly on the red felt with contrasting floss or by leaving out the flap and button.

✖ Add a few inches in width to the red felt rectangles and you'll have a cool case for your sunglasses!

frame that stitch!

Are the empty walls in your room bumming you out? Are you going to a friend's birthday party and need a super-special, one-of-a-kind gift? Have your embroidery matted and framed! It could bring new life to your room or show your friend just how much you care!

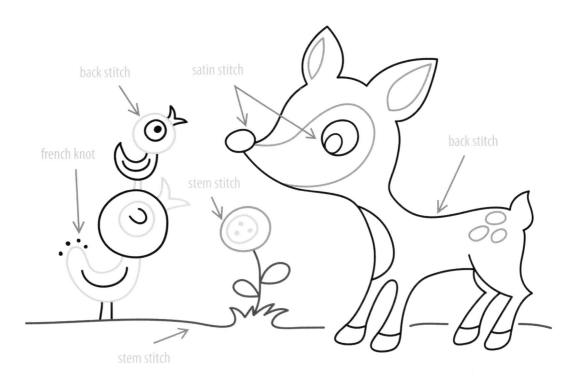

back stitch

satin stitch

french knot

stem stitch

back stitch

stem stitch

materials

You'll need:

* Picture frame with mat opening
* Piece of fabric the size of the mat
* Air-vanishing pen
* Scissors
* Embroidery hoop
* Needle
* 4 colors of floss

Step 1

Take the mat out of the frame and place it over your fabric. Trace the outer edge of the mat with an air-vanishing pen and cut out the shape along the line.

Step 2

While the mat is still on the fabric, center the deer pattern on page 75 within the mat opening. Remove the mat without moving the pattern, and then transfer the pattern onto the fabric.

another neat idea!

If you don't have a frame, you can also display your embroidery artwork in a hoop. It's inexpensive and would look great on a wall (especially if there are a few beside one another).

Center your embroidery and tighten the hoop. Cut the fabric, leaving about 1-1/2" around the hoop. Tuck the fabric behind the hoop.

Step 3

Secure your design in the center of the hoop and start stitching. Check the diagram on page 25 for color and stitch style suggestions.

Step 4

After you finish embroidering, take the design out of the hoop and place it in the frame. Now you can proudly display your embroidery or present it as a gift!

Using a running stitch, create a circle along the extra fabric that you tucked behind the hoop. Tie the ends of the floss together and hang your hoop on the wall.

jazzy jeans

Go ahead! Turn your jeans into a work of art by adding embroidered designs. It's sure to add a bounce to your step!

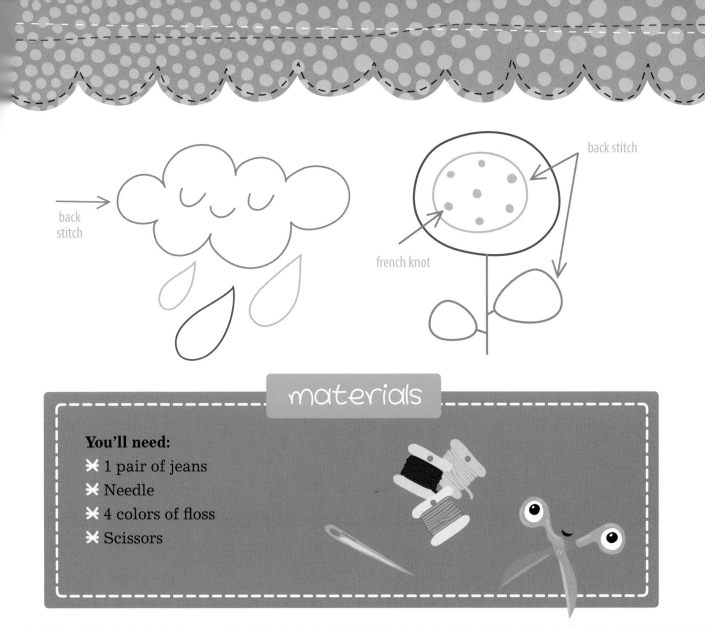

back
stitch

back stitch

french knot

materials

You'll need:

✳ 1 pair of jeans
✳ Needle
✳ 4 colors of floss
✳ Scissors

designs that will also work:

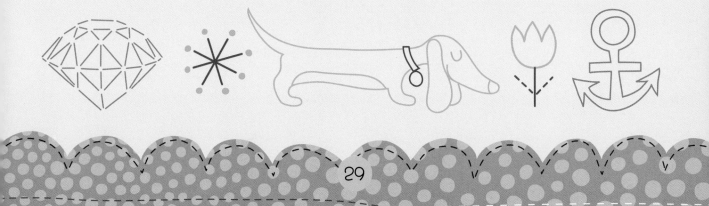

Step 1

Use one of the transferring techniques on pages 68–69 to transfer the cloud and flower designs on page 77 onto the bottom of your jeans.

Step 2

Embroider the jeans using mainly the back stitch. Use french knots for the dots inside the flower. Denim is rather stiff and sturdy, so you don't need to use the hoop.

tips

✷ Make sure that the jeans you use aren't black or very dark blue—it is difficult to see transferred patterns on dark fabric.

✷ Metallic floss can add a snazzy touch, although I suggest applying it to your back pocket. It may feel itchy against your skin.

✷ Choose simple designs and simple stitches to embroider on denim, as it's a tough fabric to penetrate.

✷ You can also do a small felt appliqué on jeans. Just cut some shapes out of felt (hearts, leaves, flowers) and use the simple running stitch to attach them to your jeans.

✷ If you have a jean skirt, jacket, or anything else denim in serious need of fun, embroider that too!

✷ Don't work too high up the pant leg or too deep into the pocket. You'll have difficulty getting your needle in and out and have a higher chance of making mistakes.

back pocket

You can also embroider the back pocket of your jeans. Choose an easy design and embroider close to the top edge of the pocket. I recommend using simple stitches, such as the back stitch, stem stitch, or split stitch. Once you've finished embroidering, you'll be ready to make a bold fashion statement in your one-of-a-kind jeans!

back stitch

pins with pizzazz

An embroidered broach
can add funky flair to
any outfit! Make pins in
different colors and have fun
accessorizing your wardrobe.

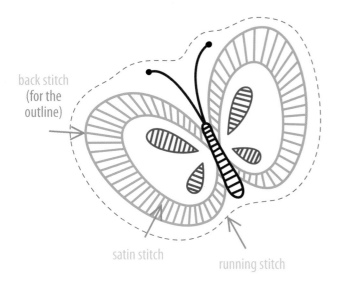

back stitch (for the outline)

satin stitch

running stitch

You'll need:
- ✳ 2 colors of felt
- ✳ Embroidery hoop
- ✳ Needle & pins
- ✳ 3 colors of floss
- ✳ Air-vanishing pen
- ✳ Scissors
- ✳ Sew-on broach pin

Step 1

This project really doesn't require much. You could even make several at the same time. Begin by transferring the butterfly design (page 79) onto the white felt. Secure your felt in the hoop and start embroidering.

Step 2

First, outline the design with a back stitch or a running stitch, and then fill in the design with a satin stitch.

Step 3

Leaving about a 1/4" space around the entire design, draw an outline with the air-vanishing pen. Take the felt out of the hoop and cut out the design along the outline. This is the front of the broach. To create the back, take the design you just cut out and place it face down on the red felt. Trace around the shape and cut it out.

designs that will also work:

Step 4

Open the broach pin and place it in the middle of the red felt piece. The broach pin should have a few holes to attach it to the felt. From the underside of the felt, push a needle through the first hole and secure the pin with two loops on each side of the hole. Repeat this step for each hole until the back of your broach resembles the picture above.

Step 5

Pin the two pieces of the broach together with the embroidered design and broach pin facing out. Now use a simple running stitch to attach the two parts.

✻ You don't have to outline your designs to create a broach. You can also center the design within a circle.

✻ These broaches can make a great Mother's Day gift!

customized card

Is there someone you'd like to thank in an extra special way?
Present them with an embroidered card, and it might
adorn their mantelpiece for a month!

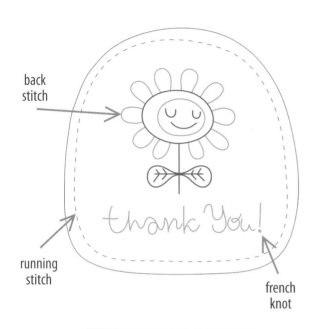

back stitch

running stitch

french knot

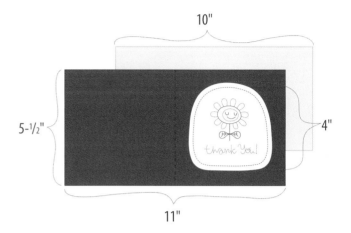

10"

5-1/2"

4"

11"

materials

You'll need:

- ✖ Cardstock
- ✖ Ruler
- ✖ Nice white paper
- ✖ Scissors
- ✖ Cotton fabric
- ✖ Embroidery hoop
- ✖ Air-vanishing pen
- ✖ 3 colors of floss
- ✖ Needle

Step 1

First, cut out a piece of cardstock 5-1/2" (W) x 11" (L), and a piece of nice white paper 5" (W) x 10" (L). Carefully fold each in half and set them aside. Transfer a pattern from page 81 onto your fabric, leaving plenty of space around your design. Put your fabric in the hoop and start embroidering.

Step 2

Embroider the design using the back stitch. You may use the stem stitch for the flower's face, but the entire design may be completed with the back stitch.

Step 3

Use the air-vanishing pen to outline the design, making sure to leave about ½" all around it. Take the fabric out of the hoop and cut along the outline. You may also cut out a 4" x 4" square around the design.

Your message here

tips

✱ You can write a message on the front of the card rather than embroidering it.

✱ Take your time embroidering on the cardstock. You don't want to end up with a bunch of unwanted holes.

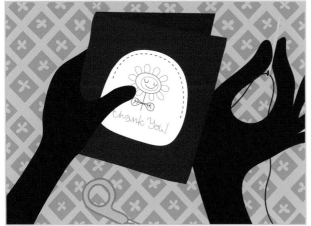

Step 4

Take the folded piece of cardstock and hold it so the opening is to the right. Place the cut-out design in the middle of the square. While holding it in place with your thumb, secure the embroidery to the cardstock with a running stitch. Take your time and be careful not to bend the cardstock.

Step 5

Now center the smaller white paper inside the piece of cardstock with the creases lined up. Use a running stitch along the middle to attach the two, making sure the end knots are hidden between the two pieces of paper. Finally, write a nice note inside your handmade card and deliver your special message.

designs that will also work:

Happy Birthday!

Yum

Hello

keepsake keychain

Place your keys on this fabulous and easy-to-make keychain, and you'll never lose them again!

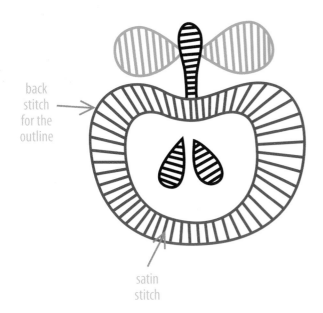

back stitch for the outline

satin stitch

Step 1

This project is very similar to the broach project, and you can easily work on several keychains at a time! Begin by transferring the pattern (page 83) onto the white felt. Put your felt into the hoop and start embroidering.

Step 2

To avoid making mistakes and to make your embroidery a bit more three-dimensional, first outline the design with a back stitch or a running stitch. Next, fill it in with the satin stitch.

Step 3

Take the design out of the hoop. Find a cup or a round object with approximately a 2" diameter. (Hint: Search the kitchen or office.) Center the design inside the circle and trace around it with the air-vanishing pen. Using the same object, make another circle on the red felt. Cut out both circles. Put the white circle on top of the red piece with the design facing out, and secure them with a couple of pins.

Your name here

designs that will also work:

Step 4

Cut 2" of ribbon, fold it in half, and place it at the top of the design with the ribbon ends between the felt circles. Secure it with a pin. This will be the loop to hold the key ring. Now using the running stitch or blanket stitch, start sewing the circles together along the outer edge.

Step 5

Pause when you have a 1" opening left, remove the pins, and add just enough stuffing to make it a bit puffy. Next, complete the running stitch circle. Create the final knot between the two felt circles and tuck it in with a needle. Attach the loop of ribbon to the key ring, and it's ready for your keys!

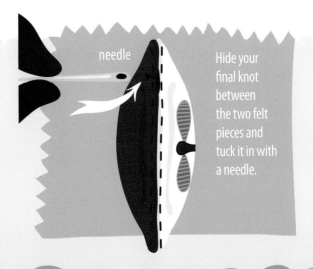

✳ Embroider your name or telephone number on the back of your keychain.

✳ Need a great gift for your BFF? Embroider a sweet little message on the back.

needle

Hide your final knot between the two felt pieces and tuck it in with a needle.

sassy
t-shirt

Do you own a plain, boring t-shirt
that's just begging for a makeover?
Give it new life with a little
embroidery design.

all in
back stitch

You'll need:
* Prewashed t-shirt
* Embroidery hoop
* Tear-away t-shirt stabilizer
* Iron
* Air-vanishing pen
* Needle
* 4 colors of floss
* Scissors

Step 1

Take an old t-shirt or a scrap of stretchy fabric, put it in a hoop, and practice a few stitches. You may want to use a tear-away t-shirt stabilizer, as it gives an extra layer of support to your fabric to prevent stretching. Ask an adult for help ironing it onto the back side of your t-shirt where you plan to embroider a design.

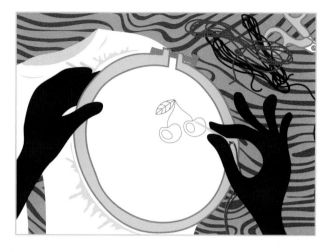

Step 2

Cut out the cherries pattern on page 85 and tape it to a window. Place your t-shirt over the design, taking your time to position it in just the right spot. Tape the t-shirt to the window, and trace the pattern onto the fabric with an air-vanishing pen.

Step 3

Center the design in a hoop. Don't tighten the hoop too much—you don't want to stretch the t-shirt. Embroider carefully (don't pull too hard) to prevent making holes in the fabric. Simple outline stitches like the back stitch and stem stitch work best. If you are going to take a break for longer than an hour, take the t-shirt out of the hoop to preserve its shape.

designs that will also work:

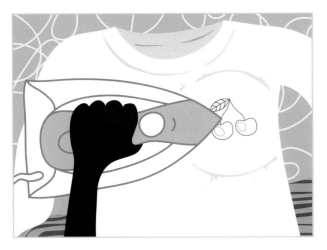

Step 4

When you finish embroidering, take the t-shirt out of the hoop and carefully tear off the stabilizer. You may want to iron out the wrinkles left by the hoop. Again, ask an adult for help. Now put on your stylish t-shirt and go show it off!

tips

✖ To decide where to place your embroidery design, try the t-shirt on and mark the spot with the air-vanishing pen. You don't want to finish the job only to find out that the design is too close to your armpit.

✖ Try to make the knots on the back as small as possible to avoid discomfort when you wear your t-shirt.

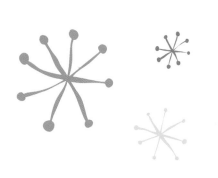

personalized pouch

A drawstring pouch is such a versatile and useful thing! You can store your jewelry, pencils, makeup, candy... virtually anything inside!

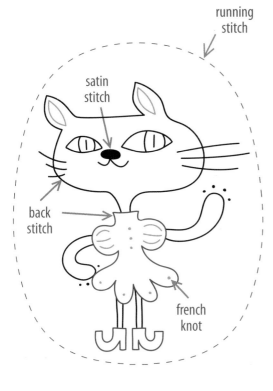

running stitch

satin stitch

back stitch

french knot

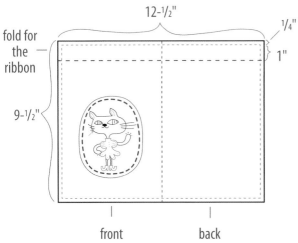

12-1/2"

fold for the ribbon

1/4"

1"

9-1/2"

front

back

materials

You'll need:

- ✳ Ruler
- ✳ 2 colors of cotton fabric
- ✳ Scissors
- ✳ Iron
- ✳ Sewing needle & thread
- ✳ Needle & pins
- ✳ 3 colors of floss
- ✳ Embroidery hoop
- ✳ Air-vanishing pen
- ✳ 20" ribbon
- ✳ Safety pin
- ✳ Felt

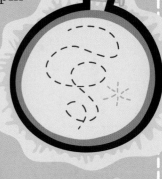

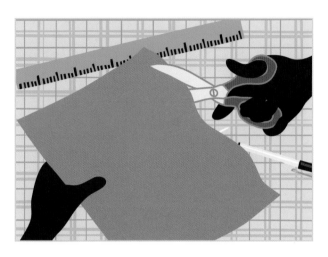

Step 1

Measure and cut a rectangle of pink fabric 9-1/2" (W) x 12-1/2" (L).

Step 2

Next, fold in all the edges by 1/4" and iron them down to make hemming easier. Ask an adult for assistance. With pink sewing thread, hem the edges using a running stitch.

Step 3

Now fold down the top 1" of fabric. Stitch the two sides together with floss, leaving a 3/4" space for the ribbon.

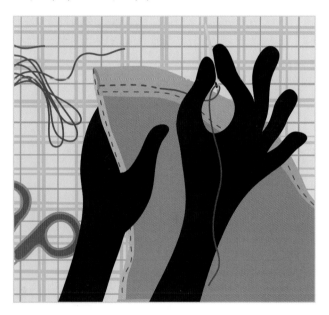

Step 4

Take a piece of white cotton fabric, transfer on the design from page 87, and center it in a hoop. Embroider the design using the back stitch for a nice continuous line. Fill in the nose with the satin stitch, and use french knots for the buttons and cat's paws. After completing the embroidery, draw a shape around it with the air-vanishing pen and cut it out.

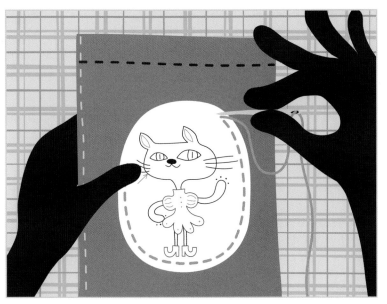

Step 5

Next, fold the hemmed fabric rectangle in half so the hemmed edges are hidden inside. Place your embroidered appliqué in the middle and secure it with pins. Using the running stitch, sew the design onto the hemmed piece, but be sure to only attach the appliqué to one layer of the fabric.

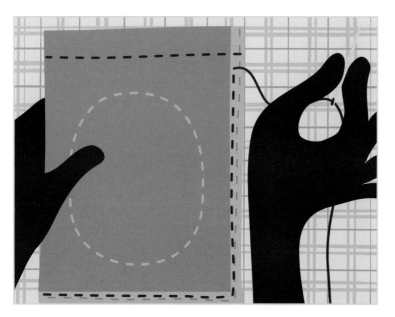

Step 6

Now fold the project the other way, with the design facing in and the hemming facing out. Using the simple running stitch and sewing thread, sew the bottom and the open side together. Leave the top 1" for the ribbon opening. Next, push the bottom of the pouch up and out through the top so that the design is facing out and the hemming is hidden inside.

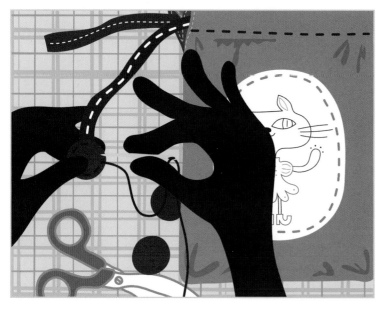

Step 7

Take a 20" piece of ribbon and attach a safety pin to the end. Insert the safety pin into one loop opening, and carefully push and pull the fabric to get the safety pin out the other end. Remove the safety pin and tie knots at the ends of the ribbon. For more pizzazz, cut out four felt circles with 1" diameters. Sandwich each end of the ribbon between two circles and secure them with pins. Using the running stitch, sew the circles to the ribbon ends. Now you're good to go!

purr-fect!

tips

✳ You can make the pouch any size you want. Make one big enough to fit your lunch or even your gym shoes. Make a tiny one to store your jewelry and makeup. A pouch is a pouch!

✳ To save time, embroider directly on the pouch. Just be sure to choose floss in colors that show up well against your fabric.

holiday ornaments

Searching for ways to spruce up your tree, or thinking of creating cute little gifts? These appliqué ornaments will add a cozy charm to your holiday festivities!

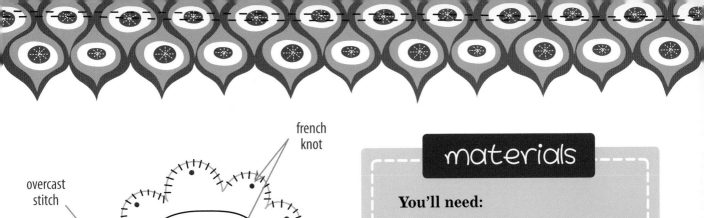

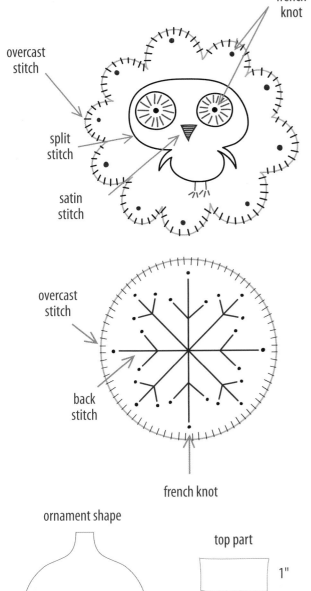

french knot

overcast
stitch

split
stitch

satin
stitch

overcast
stitch

back
stitch

french knot

ornament shape

top part

1"

2"

materials

You'll need:

✳ 3 colors of felt
✳ Embroidery hoop
✳ Needle & pins
✳ 3 colors of floss
✳ Scissors
✳ Stuffing
✳ 12" ribbon

Step 1

Transfer the designs on page 89 onto two pieces of white felt. Embroider each design with the felt secured in the hoop using the stitches (except the overcast) indicated in the diagrams at left.

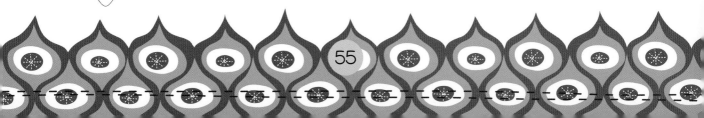

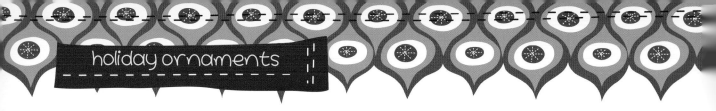

Step 2

Cut out the embroidery designs, and set aside these appliqués for now. Next, draw the ornament shape onto red and green felt pieces and cut them out. Secure each appliqué to the center of an ornament-shaped felt piece with pins.

Step 3

Attach the appliqués to the red and green felt pieces using the overcast stitch. Next, put the two pieces back-to-back, so the embroidery designs face out, and secure them with pins.

Step 4

Use the overcast stitch to sew the two sides together, but leave a 2" opening for the stuffing. Insert just enough stuffing to make your ornament puffy.

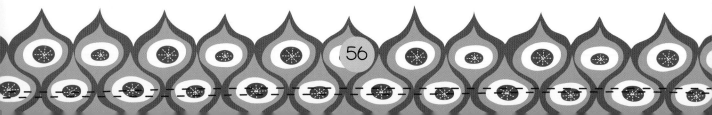

Step 5

Now, cut out a rectangle 1" (W) x 2" (L) from white felt. Fold it in half over the top ¹⁄₂" of the ornament and secure it with a pin. Attach the white top to the ornament using the simple running stitch in a U shape. Be sure to leave ¹⁄₂" at the top on both sides unstitched for the ribbon. Cut 12" of ribbon and slip the ribbon through the ornament top. Tie a pretty bow at the ends, and your ornament is ready!

tips

✷ Try cutting your ornament in different shapes, or embroider directly onto the ornament piece without using an appliqué.

✷ To save time, just add an embroidery design to one side of your ornament.

toasty scarf

Add a splash of color and individuality to your winter wardrobe, and stay warm and toasty with this embroidered fleece scarf!

satin stitch

running stitch

back stitch

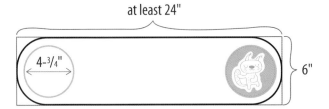

at least 24"

4-³/₄"

6"

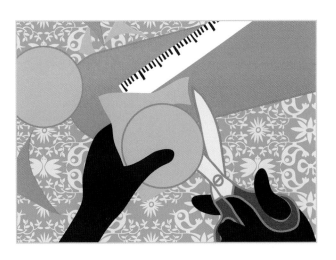

Step 1

Measure and cut a rectangle of orange fleece measuring 6" (W) x (at least) 24" (L). Round off the corners so the ends of your scarf are semicircles. Now, cut out two circles measuring 4-³/4" in diameter from the yellow fleece.

Step 2

Transfer the two characters from the top of page 91 onto white fleece. Embroider the designs using the back stitch for the outlines, the satin stitch for the noses, and the running stitch for the bellies and inside the ears.

Step 3

Outline the finished embroidered characters with the air-vanishing pen, leaving about 1/4" around them. Carefully cut out the characters.

designs that will also work:

Step 4

Next, center the designs on the fleece circles and secure them in place with pins. Using the overcast stitch and white floss, attach the characters to the two circles.

Step 5

Finally, place a circle on each end of the scarf (at least ½" from the bottom) and secure them with pins. Attach the circles to the scarf using a simple running stitch. Now you are ready to face the winter chill!

✻ You can simplify this project by embroidering directly onto the fleece circles or scarf ends.

✻ You can also add an embroidered appliqué, or embroider directly onto a scarf that you already own.

✻ If you can bear to part with it, this scarf makes an excellent gift!

hipster headband

Keep your ears warm and your mane tame with this chic and stylish winter headband. Go ahead, make one for yourself and one for your BFF.

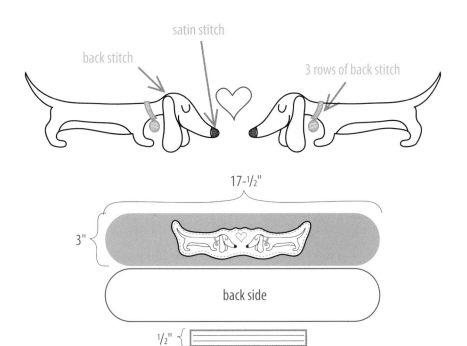

back stitch

satin stitch

3 rows of back stitch

17-½"

3"

back side

½"

4"

materials

You'll need:

* 3 colors of fleece fabric
* Ruler
* Scissors
* Air-vanishing pen
* 4" of ½"-wide elastic
* Embroidery hoop
* Needle & pins
* 3 colors of floss

Step 1

Measure and cut a rectangle of yellow fleece measuring 3" (W) x 17-1/2" (L). Round off the corners so the ends of your headband are semicircles.

Step 2

Place the cut piece onto the orange fleece and trace it with the air-vanishing pen.

Step 3

Carefully cut the headband shape out of the orange piece of felt. Next, cut a 4"-long piece of elastic and set it aside.

Step 4

Transfer the dog and heart patterns (page 93) onto the white fleece. You'll be able to fit only half of the design in the hoop at a time, so complete one half, and then adjust the design in the hoop to embroider the other dog. Use the back stitch for the outlines and eyes, the satin stitch for the noses, and a few back-to-back rows of back stitch to fill in the leashes.

Step 5

Outline your embroidery with the air-vanishing pen, leaving a 1/2" space around the entire design. Carefully cut out your appliqué.

tips

✳ Simplify this project by embroidering directly onto the top layer of the headband with contrasting floss colors.

✳ Make your headband narrower or wider, depending on your preference.

Step 6

Next, place the embroidered design in the middle of the yellow felt and secure it in place with pins. Using the running stitch, sew the two pieces together.

Step 7

Place the two sides of the headband together with the design facing out. Insert 1/2" of elastic between the fabric pieces at one end of the headband. Secure everything with pins, and start sewing the two pieces together using the running stitch. Insert the other end of the elastic 1/2" deep between the fleece pieces at the opposite end of the headband to complete the circle. Add a few extra stitches over the elastic parts.

designs that will also work:

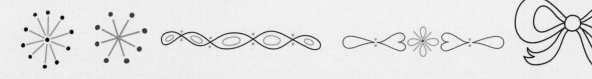

templates

You are welcome to create your own designs, drawing them directly on the fabric with a fabric pen. However, if you use the templates in this book or prefer to draw your design on a separate piece of paper before applying it to your project, you need to use one of the following transfer techniques. Try using a window, as this is the simplest method. With thicker or darker fabrics, use the basting or carbon paper methods.

materials

You'll need:
* A pattern
* Tape
* Fabric
* Air-vanishing pen
* A window or a light table

using a window

This transfer technique works best with thin, light-colored fabric.

Step 1
Secure your pattern onto the window or light table with tape.

Step 2
Place your fabric on top of the pattern and secure it with tape on all four sides (so it doesn't move while you are tracing it).

Step 3
Using an air-vanishing pen, trace your design onto the fabric.

basting

This method works well for transferring simple patterns onto felt and other thick, fuzzy fabrics.

1. Draw or trace a design onto tracing paper or tissue paper.
2. Place the paper on top of your fabric and secure it with pins.
3. Using a loose running stitch, "baste" (or stitch over) the design onto the fabric with sewing thread that is the same color as your floss, creating a color-coded pattern to follow.
4. Tear away the paper. You may want to soften the paper by soaking it in water before removing it.

carbon paper

For light-colored fabric, you can use pencil carbon paper. However, you may need to use dressmaker's carbon for darker fabric.

1. Put a sheet of carbon paper (carbon side down) between the design and fabric. You may want to place a piece of fine-grain sandpaper beneath your fabric to prevent the fabric from moving around or bunching up.
2. Go over the design with a pencil or pen, pressing firmly enough to transfer the design onto the fabric. Be careful not to rub the carbon paper against the fabric, as it may produce smudges.

69

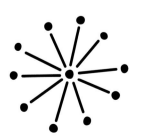

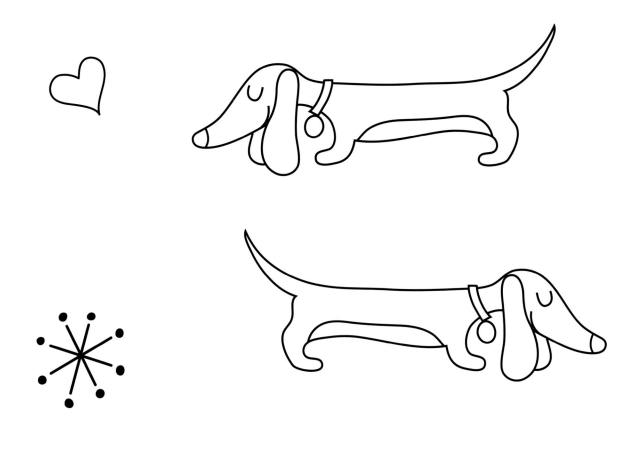

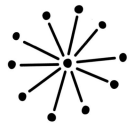

About the Author

A resident of Ottawa, Ontario, Canada, Helen Dardik is a versatile artist, dividing her creative energies between illustration, crafting, and oil painting. Everything Helen sees inspires her, especially her children's drawings, which come from "the ultimate source—infinite imagination." In her spare time, Helen makes plush toys, rearranges furniture, and drinks gallons of coffee while flipping through design magazines to spark new ideas. She also enjoys traveling with her girls and husband. Other career paths Helen has considered include taste testing candy, opera singing, and cake decorating!

Acknowledgments

Many thanks to my wonderful family for putting up with my all-consuming addiction to arts and crafts.

All my best,

Helen

Editor: Heidi Kellenberger
Associate Editor: Sandy Phan
Art Direction: Shelley Baugh and David Rosemeyer
Photography: Creative Publishing Photo Studio
Production Design: Debbie Aiken
Production Management: Irene Chan, Rushi Sanathra, and
Nicole Szawlowski
Publisher: Pauline Molinari